Basic Skills
Map Skills

Grade 3

by

Jan Kennedy

Published by Instructional Fair
an imprint of
Frank Schaffer Publications®

Instructional Fair

Author: Jan Kennedy
Editors: Rhonda DeWaard, Sue Vanderlaan, Lisa Hancock
Cover Artist: Matthew Van Zomeren
Interior Designer: Pat Geasler
Interior Artist: Pat Biggs
Photo Credits: ©GlobeShots™, ©Cartesia Software, ©Visual Language

Frank Schaffer Publications®

Instructional Fair is an imprint of Frank Schaffer Publications.

Send all inquiries to:
Frank Schaffer Publications
3195 Wilson Drive NW
Grand Rapids, Michigan 49534

Map Skills—grade 3

ISBN: 1-56822-638-1

8 9 10 PAT 08 07 06

Table of Contents

Which Way Is Up?

Name _____

Label the direction each arrow is pointing on the matching line. Use **N, E, S, W, NE, SE, NW, SW**. Then color the arrows as directed in the Color Code Box.

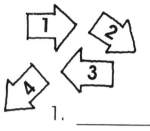

1. _____
2. _____
3. _____
4. _____

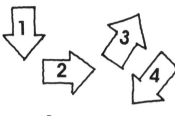

1. _____
2. _____
3. _____
4. _____

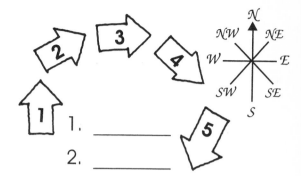

1. _____
2. _____
3. _____
4. _____
5. _____

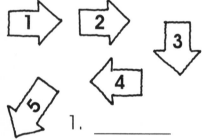

1. _____
2. _____
3. _____
4. _____
5. _____

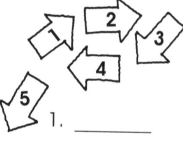

1. _____
2. _____
3. _____
4. _____
5. _____

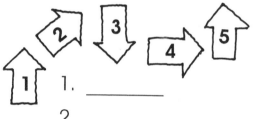

1. _____
2. _____
3. _____
4. _____
5. _____

1. _____
2. _____
3. _____
4. _____
5. _____
6. _____

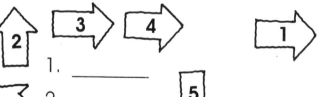

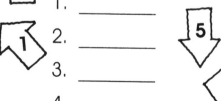

1. _____
2. _____
3. _____
4. _____
5. _____
6. _____

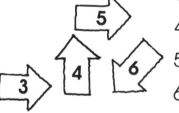

Color Code Box

N—red	**W**—brown
NE—blue	**NW**—orange
S—green	**SW**—yellow
SE—pink	**E**—purple

IF5190 *Map Skills*

Dizzy Designers

Name _____

Decorate the compass rose boxes by following the directions below.

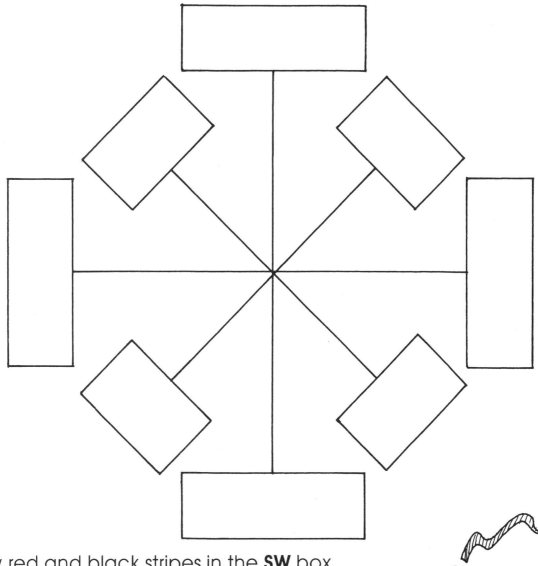

1. Draw red and black stripes in the **SW** box.

2. Draw 3 green triangles in the **N** box.

3. Make the **E** box red and blue plaid.

4. Draw purple polka dots in the **NW** box.

5. Make orange wavy lines in the **SE** box.

6. Draw two red squares in the **S** box.

7. Draw green diagonal lines in the **W** box.

8. Make two yellow smiling faces in the **NE** box.

Space Ship Search

Name _____

Gus Galactic needs help in identifying these alien spaceships. Write a ship's letter in each blank to solve these riddles.

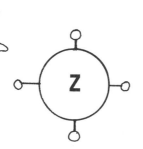

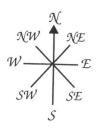
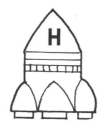
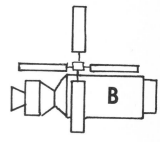
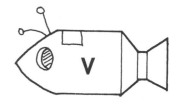

1. I am **N** of Ship **H**. _____

2. I am **E** of Ship **Z**. _____

3. I am **SE** of Ship **Z**. _____

4. I am **S** of Ship **O**. _____

5. I am **NW** of Ship **Z**. _____

6. I am **SW** of Ship **B**. _____

7. I am **NE** of Ship **Z**. _____

8. I am **NE** of Ship **I**. _____

9. I am **SE** of Ship **U**. _____

10. I am **NW** of Ship **B**. _____

Cosmic Challenge

Start at Ship **H**. Travel in the orbit given. Which ship will you dock with?

1. Go **NW** to Ship _____ .

2. Go **NE** to Ship _____ .

3. Go **NE** to Ship _____ .

4. Go **S** to Ship _____ .

5. Go **SE** to Ship _____ .

6. Go **NE** to Ship _____ .

7. Go **NW** to Ship _____ .

This is your docking station. Congratulations!

It's a Strike!

Name _____

Don't let these map terms bowl you over! Follow the compass rose directions. Write down the letter on each pin that you bowl down to form a map term. Start with the circled pin.

E

1. Move **NE** to _____
2. Move **SE** to _____
3. Move **SW** to _____
4. Move **SW** to _____
5. Move **NW** to _____
6. Move **NW** to _____

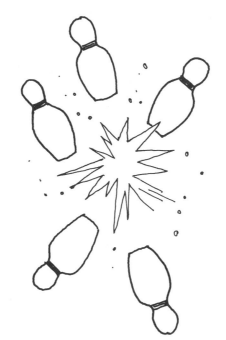

C

1. Move **SE** to _____
2. Move **E** to _____
3. Move **NE** to _____
4. Move **W** to _____
5. Move **NW** to _____
6. Move **E** to _____
7. Move **E** to _____
8. Move **SW** to _____

L

1. Move **E** to _____
2. Move **E** to _____
3. Move **E** to _____
4. Move **SW** to _____
5. Move **SW** to _____
6. Move **NW** to _____
7. Move **SW** to _____

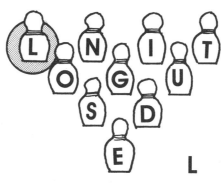

L

1. Move **SE** to _____
2. Move **NE** to _____
3. Move **SE** to _____
4. Move **NE** to _____
5. Move **E** to _____
6. Move **SW** to _____
7. Move **SW** to _____
8. Move **SW** to _____

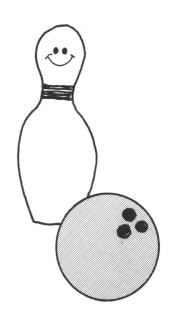

Stocking Sports Shelves Name _____

Identify the grid box location for the following items in the Sports-R-Us Shop.

	1	**2**	**3**	**4**	**5**	**6**	**7**	**8**
A	baseball		whistle	golf tee	cleats		goggles	
B		barbell		volleyball		hockey stick		basketball
C	goal post	football			referee jersey			bat
D			golf club			basketball net	tennis racquet	
E	soccer ball		hockey net	mitt				tennis ball

1. golf ball and tee   *A-4*   11. whistle _____

2. catcher's mitt _____   12. cleats _____

3. basketball _____   13. golf club _____

4. referee jersey _____   14. tennis racquet _____

5. volleyball _____   15. football _____

6. tennis ball _____   16. barbell _____

7. goal post _____   17. soccer ball _____

8. swimming goggles _____   18. hockey stick _____

9. hockey goal net _____   19. baseball _____

10. baseball bat _____   20. basketball net _____

Fill in these grids with your . . .

     D-1   first name   A-8   last name   C-7   favorite sport

     C-3   school's name   D-4   favorite number   E-6   favorite color

Terrific Treats!

Name _____

Create a food map by drawing the foods in the grid as directed.

	1	2	3	4	5	6	7
A							
B							
C							
D							
E							

1. carrot C–1
2. orange B–1
3. pizza E–1
4. birthday cake C–5
5. glass of milk D–5
6. apple A–3
7. chocolate chip cookie E–7
8. hamburger B–6
9. chocolate kisses C–2
10. banana D–1
11. can of soda pop E–5
12. piece of bread A–4
13. candy bar B–7
14. cupcake C–6
15. bacon E–3
16. eggs E–2
17. lollipop D–4
18. ice-cream bar A–5

19. M&Ms B–2
20. Cheerios A–1
21. grapes A–7
22. hot dog D–6
23. head of lettuce D–3
24. cherry pie D–7
25. grapefruit B–3
26. can of soup E–6
27. French fries A–6
28. pretzel C–4
29. peanut B–4
30. drumstick C–3
31. ice-cream cone E–4
32. popcorn B–5
33. fish A–2
34. strawberry D–2
35. candy cane C–7

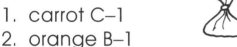
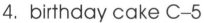

The Grid Name Game   Name _____

Cut out the squares. Glue each onto the correct grid map section. Then above the page title at the top of the page write the coordinates that spell your name.

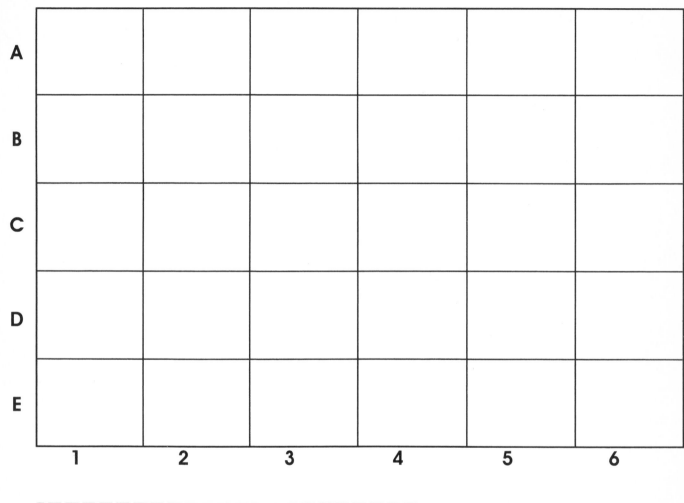

 # World Map

Name _____

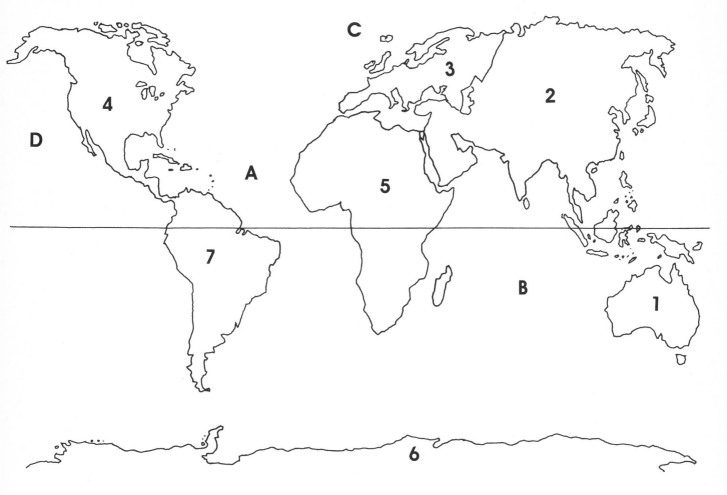

Name the continents as numbered on the map.

1. _____

2. _____

3. _____

4. _____

5. _____

6. _____

7. _____

Name the oceans as lettered on the map.

A. _____

B. _____

C. _____

D. _____

Color the equator red.

Outline all of the continents in green.

Draw one blue fish in each ocean.

The Puzzle Planet

Name _____

Color the continents as directed in the key. Cut them out. Then cut out ocean labels and the key. Glue all pieces onto blue paper in the proper places.

Pacific	Atlantic	Indian	Arctic

Key

North America—red   Africa—tan
South America—yellow   Antarctica—white
Europe—orange   Australia—green
                          Asia—purple

Globe Puzzle

Name _____

Use a world map to solve this puzzle.

Europe   equator
Australia axis
Africa   north
Asia   south
Pacific   continents
Indian   North America
Atlantic South America
Arctic   Antarctica

Across
2. U.S.A.'s continent
3. southernmost continent
5. opposite north
6. continent west of Asia
8. divides the earth into northern and southern hemispheres
9. island continent
11. earth "spins" on it
12. largest ocean
13. ocean east of Africa

Down
1. large continent northeast of Africa
2. direction of the North Pole from the equator
4. continent between the Atlantic and Indian Oceans
5. Brazil's continent
7. land masses of earth
10. ocean east of North America
11. northernmost ocean

 Global Fun

A globe is a model of the earth. Complete the globe by following the directions below.

1. Draw a whale in the southern hemisphere part of the Pacific Ocean.

2. Trace the equator in orange.

3. Draw a shark in the Arctic Ocean.

4. Draw a smile face near Antarctica.

5. Draw an ocean liner in the northern hemisphere part of the Atlantic Ocean.

6. Color the axis poles red.

7. In North America, color Mexico yellow, Canada green, and the U.S.A. red.

8. Draw a yellow **X** in the northern hemisphere part of Africa.

9. Color Europe purple.

10. Draw rainbow-colored diagonal stripes on South America.

11. Draw orange polka dots on Asia.

12. Draw an orange circle on the southern hemisphere part of Africa.

Happy Hemispheres

Name _____

Write the name of each continent and ocean next to its number.

Western Hemisphere

Eastern Hemisphere

Word Bank

Atlantic
Pacific
Indian
Arctic
North America
South America
Europe
Australia
Asia
Africa
Antarctica

1. _____

2. _____

3. _____

4. _____

1. _____

2. _____

3. _____

4. _____

5. _____

6. _____

Southern Hemisphere

Northern Hemisphere

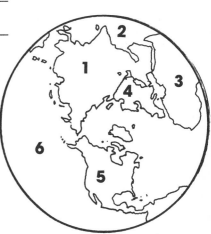

1. _____

2. _____

3. _____

4. _____

5. _____

6. _____

1. _____

2. _____

3. _____

4. _____   6. _____

5. _____   7. _____

Wavy Water World

Name _____

Welcome to Wavy Water World! Draw your own symbols for the places listed in the map key. Then place them on the map as directed.

Wavy Water World

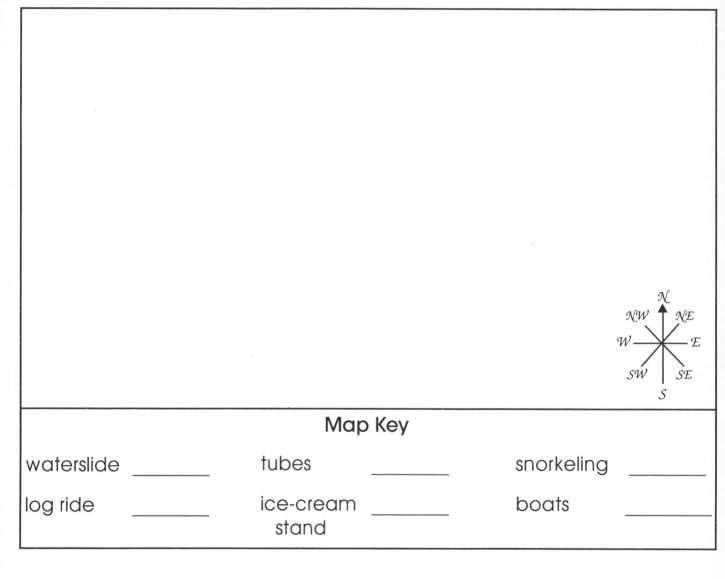

Map Key

waterslide	_____	tubes	_____	snorkeling	_____
log ride	_____	ice-cream stand	_____	boats	_____

1. Draw 4 waterslides in the northeast corner of the park.

2. Draw tubes in the center of the park from the north to the south edges.

3. Draw snorkeling in the southwest corner.

4. Draw the ice-cream stand south of the waterslides.

5. Draw 5 boats in the northwest corner of the park.

6. Draw the log ride on the west side, between boats and snorkeling.

Kool Kids Mall

Name _____

Mall Map

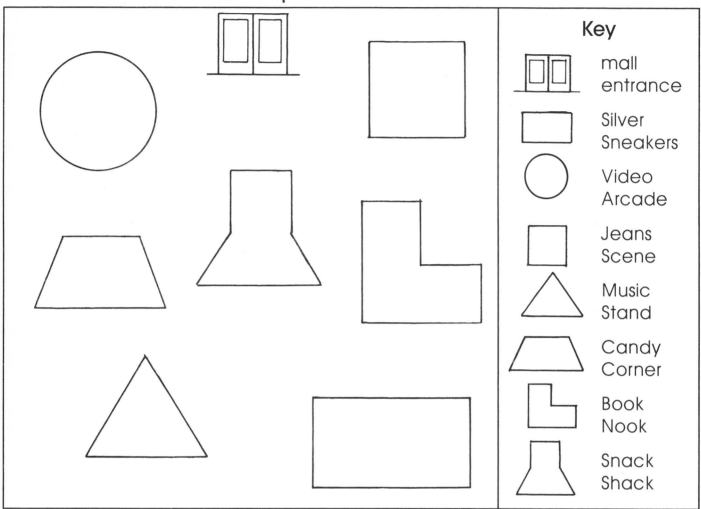

Key

mall entrance
Silver Sneakers
Video Arcade
Jeans Scene
Music Stand
Candy Corner
Book Nook
Snack Shack

Use the key to locate the stores. Draw the following:

1. a red and blue athletic shoe in Silver Sneakers

2. a black musical note in the Music Stand

3. a pair of blue jeans in the Jeans Scene

4. a green tree on each side of the mall entrance

5. a red piece of pizza in the Snack Shack

6. a pair of eyeballs in the Video Arcade

7. a yellow and blue book in the Book Nook

8. an orange lollipop in the Candy Corner

My Home Town

Name _____

Complete the map by drawing the symbols from the key by each matching number on the map.

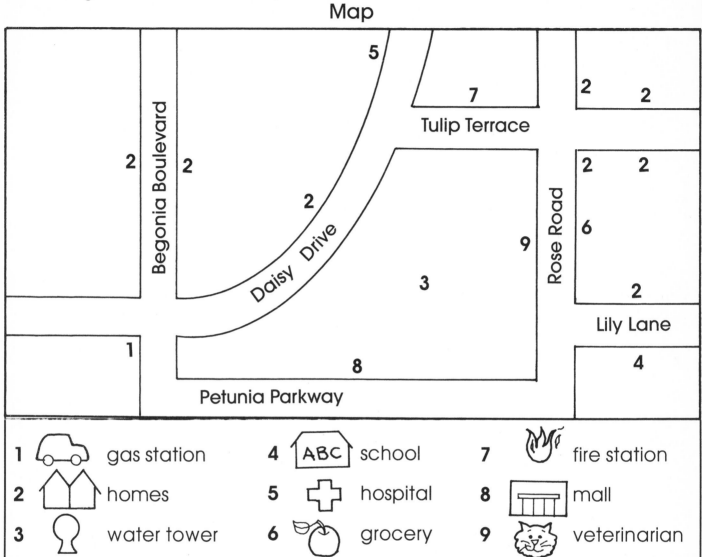

Name the streets.

1. The gas station is on the corner of _____ and _____ .

2. The vet is on _____ .

3. The fire station is on _____ .

4. There are no homes on _____ .

5. The school is on _____ .

6. The grocery is on _____ .

State Smart

Name _____

Map

Use this map of some of the states to answer the questions below.

Lake Superior

Lake Huron

Lake Michigan

MICHIGAN

Detroit

Grand Rapids •

Lansing ★

Lake Erie

PENNSYLVANIA

Chicago •

Cleveland •

Fort Wayne •

Pittsburgh •

Harrisburg ★

ILLINOIS

Springfield ★

Indianapolis ★

OHIO

Columbus ★

Philadelphia •

INDIANA

Cincinnati •

Charleston ★

Ohio R.

WEST VIRGINIA

Louisville •

★ Frankfort

KENTUCKY

Key
★ state capital
• city
~ river
--- state

1. What state is west of Ohio? _____

2. The capital of West Virginia is _____ .

3. Pittsburgh is a city in the state of _____ .

4. What Ohio city is on the Ohio River? _____

5. Which state is southwest of Michigan? _____

6. What lake is west of Michigan? _____

7. Frankfort is the capital of _____ .

8. What is the capital of Indiana? _____

9. Springfield is the capital of _____ .

10. Chicago is _____ of Springfield, Illinois.

11. What Ohio city is northeast of Columbus? _____

12. Grand Rapids is _____ of Lansing, Michigan.

13. What state is east of Illinois? _____

14. What lake forms the northern border of Ohio? _____

Mixed-Up Map Maker

Name _____

Mattie Map Maker goofed when creating a map of the state of Oopsylvania. Circle in color her mistakes and put a number by each one. Then describe each error on the line with the matching number. (**Hint:** The key shows the correct map symbols.)

Oopsylvania Map

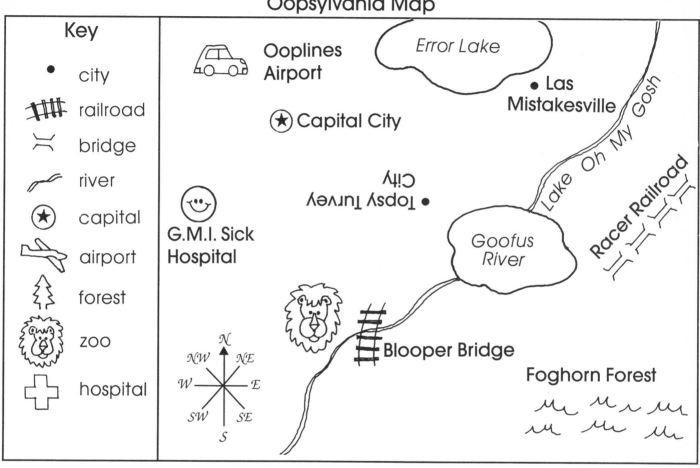

1. _____

2. _____

3. _____

4. _____

5. _____

6. _____

7. _____

8. _____

Creating a Map

Name _____

Pretend you are looking at your school classroom from high atop the lighting fixtures. Draw how your classroom looks. Include a key to explain the symbols you draw.

Key

⊕ Delivery Dilemma

Name _____

Carrie lost her way while delivering the mail. Follow the directions to help her complete her route.

Carrie's Map

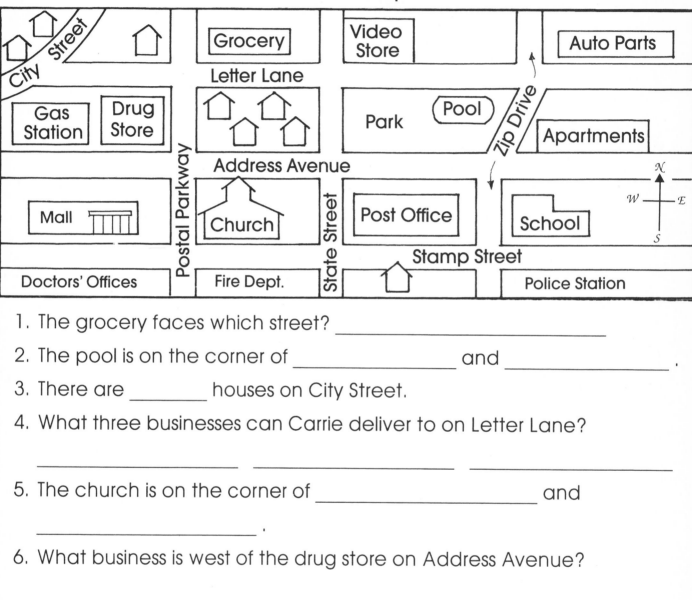

1. The grocery faces which street? _____

2. The pool is on the corner of _____ and _____ .

3. There are _____ houses on City Street.

4. What three businesses can Carrie deliver to on Letter Lane?

   _____   _____   _____

5. The church is on the corner of _____ and

   _____ .

6. What business is west of the drug store on Address Avenue?

   _____

7. To get from the church to City Street, Carrie would go north on

   _____ , then west on _____ .

8. The post office is on a block bordered by which four streets?

   _____   _____

   _____   _____

A Real "Moose-tery"

Name _____

Horrible Harvey Hunter has disappeared somewhere in the Mysterious Moosehead Mansion. Detective Dimwitt is trying to find him. Use the key to identify rooms in the mansion. Then use a pencil to trace the route Detective Dimwitt took to locate the hapless Harvey.

Moosehead Mansion Map

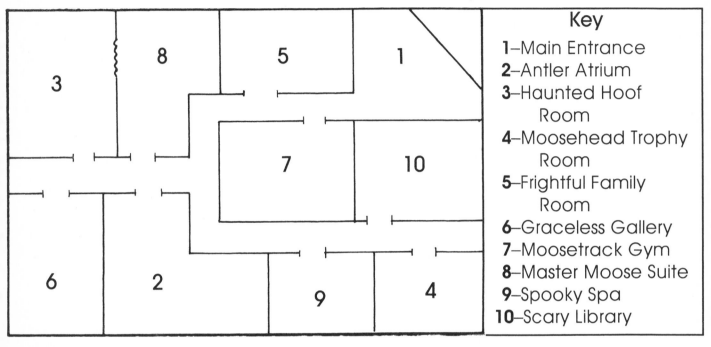

Key

1–Main Entrance
2–Antler Atrium
3–Haunted Hoof Room
4–Moosehead Trophy Room
5–Frightful Family Room
6–Graceless Gallery
7–Moosetrack Gym
8–Master Moose Suite
9–Spooky Spa
10–Scary Library

Detective Dimwitt's Route

1. He enters the mansion at the Main Entrance.

2. Next he checks out the Moosetrack Gym.

3. Then he sneaks down the hall to the Antler Atrium.

4. From there he checks the Spooky Spa.

5. No luck, so on to the Scary Library he goes.

6. Next, the detective scans the Moosehead Trophy Room.

7. Then he walks along the hall to look in the Frightful Family Room.

8. No Harvey there, so he moves on to the Graceless Gallery.

9. Could he be in the Master Moose Suite? He checks there.

10. Then he looks in the Haunted Hoof Room.

11. There he discovers a secret room. Inside he finds Harvey reading a hunting magazine. The search is over!

Color My World

Name _____

Color each gumball as directed in the Color Key.

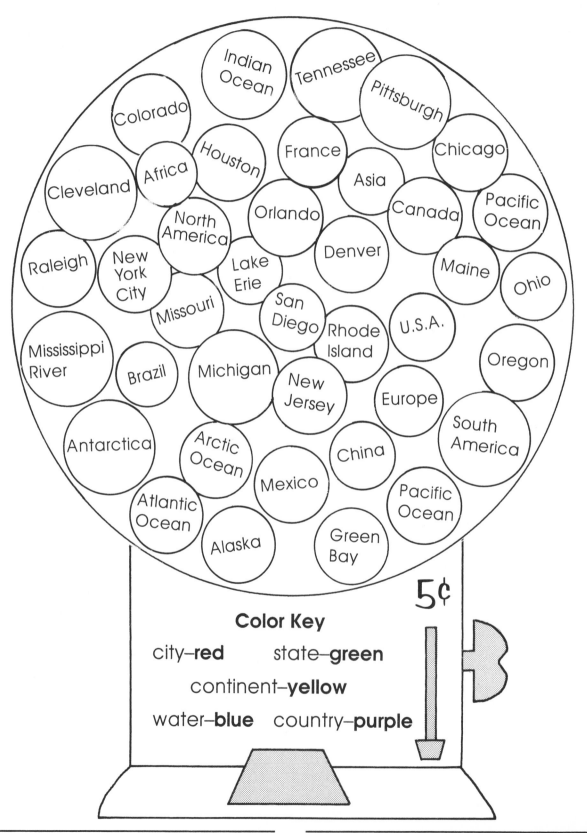

Color Key

city–**red**   state–**green**

continent–**yellow**

water–**blue**   country–**purple**

5¢

Natural Wonders

Name _____

Earth's physical features are its natural formations. Match each formation with its definition by writing a number in each blank.

____	river	1. land rising high above the land around it
____	bay	2. land surrounded completely by water
____	island	3. piece of land surrounded by water on all but one side
____	gulf	4. inlet of a large water body that extends into the land; smaller than a gulf
____	mountain	5. Earth opening that spills lava, rock, and gases
____	plain	6. large inland body of water
____	lake	7. lowland between hills or mountains
____	peninsula	8. long, narrow body of water
____	valley	9. large area of flat grasslands
____	volcano	10. vast body of salt water
____	ocean	11. large area of a sea or ocean partially enclosed by land

Now write each feature's number on the map.

Features Map

 # Land Regions

Name _____

Physical maps show natural features of the earth such as water, mountains, deserts, and high and low regions. Finish the map as directed.

Physical Map

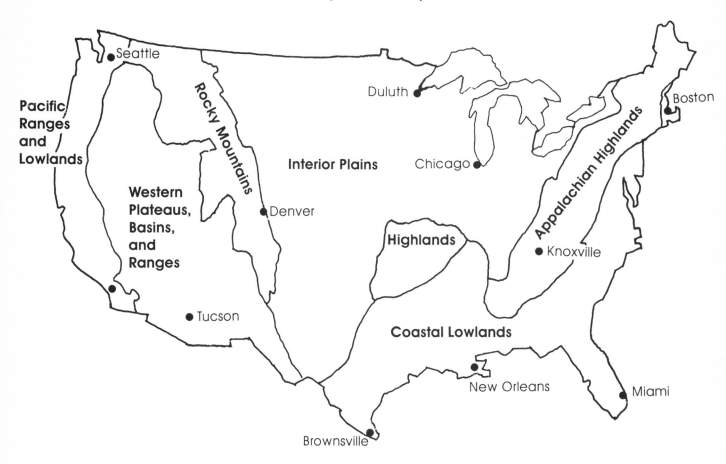

1. Draw brown ⌒⌒ in the mountain and highland regions.

2. Draw orange ⊒⁼⊒ on the Pacific Ranges and Lowlands.

3. Color the 5 Great Lakes blue.

4. Draw green ᨬᨬᨬ on the Coastal Lowlands.

5. Draw red ////////// in the Western Plateaus, Basins, and Ranges.

6. Color the Interior Plains yellow.

7. Name one city found in the mountains. _____

8. Name one city found in the Coastal Lowlands. _____

Northern Neighbors

Name _____

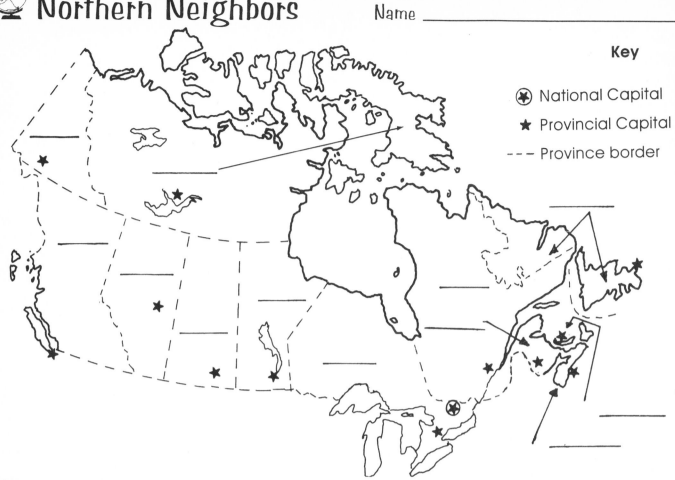

Key

⊛ National Capital
★ Provincial Capital
--- Province border

Write each province or territory name abbreviation by the correct blank on the map.

1. British Columbia   (B.C.)
2. Alberta   (Alta.)
3. Saskatchewan   (Sask.)
4. Manitoba   (Man.)
5. Ontario   (Ont.)
6. Quebec   (Que.)
7. Newfoundland   (Nfld.)
8. New Brunswick   (N.B.)
9. Nova Scotia   (N.S.)
10. Prince Edward Island (P.E.I.)
11. Northwest Territories   (N.W.T.)
12. Yukon Territory   (Y.T.)

Answer these questions.

1. Which province is north of the Great Lakes? _____

2. Which province contains the national capital? _____

3. What province is east of British Columbia? _____

4. What province is southeast of New Brunswick? _____

5. Manitoba is _____ of Saskatchewan.

Scale Is Fun!

Name _____

A scale measures distance on a map. Use the scale given to measure distances in this winter wonderland. Cut out the ruler. Use it to measure from ✳ to ✳ to answer the questions below.

Scale

0 _____ 1

1 inch = 10 feet

1. On the scale, how many feet equal one inch? _____

2. How far is it from the shovel to the sleigh? _____

3. How many feet is the snow angel from the snowman? _____

4. How far is the igloo from the sleigh? _____

5. How many feet is it from the snowmobile to the skis and poles? _____

6. How many feet is the snow fort from the shovel? _____

7. It is _____ feet from the sledding hill to the shovel.

8. It is _____ feet from the skis and pole to the sleigh.

9. It is _____ feet from the skis and pole to the igloo.

| 1 inch | 2 inches | 3 inches | 4 inches | 5 inches | 6 inches |

New Neighbors for Nelly Name _____

Nelly and her family have just moved to their new farm. How far will Nelly have to travel to meet her new neighbors? Cut out the ruler and use to measure the distances. Be sure to check the scale given on the map. Measure from • to •.

Nelly's Map

1. Nelly first met Barb, who lived _____ miles away.

2. The next day she rode on her bike to meet Tim, who lived _____ miles away.

3. The next day Pat came over to Nelly's. She lived _____ miles away.

4. Nelly and Pat then went to meet Lisa, who lived _____ miles away.

5. The next day Nelly rode her bike for _____ miles to meet Megan.

6. From Megan's, she rode to Brent's house which was _____ miles.

7. From Brent's she rode _____ miles to meet Craig.

Flight Path Frenzy

Name _____

You are the new National
Airlines navigator. Use the scale
to measure the approximate distance of these flights.
Draw the flight paths using the colors stated.

Scale

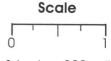

0   1

1 inch = 200 miles

From:

1. Atlanta to Dallas _____ miles (orange)

2. Denver to Chicago _____ miles (purple)

3. Los Angeles to Phoenix _____ miles (yellow)

4. Seattle to Dallas _____ miles (green)

5. St. Louis to New York _____ miles (brown)

6. Denver to Miami _____ miles (red)

7. Reno to Detroit _____ miles (dark blue)

8. Los Angeles to New York _____ miles (pink)

9. Seattle to St. Louis _____ miles (black)

10. Chicago to Miami _____ miles (light blue)

IF5190 *Map Skills*

Boundary Bonanza

Name _____

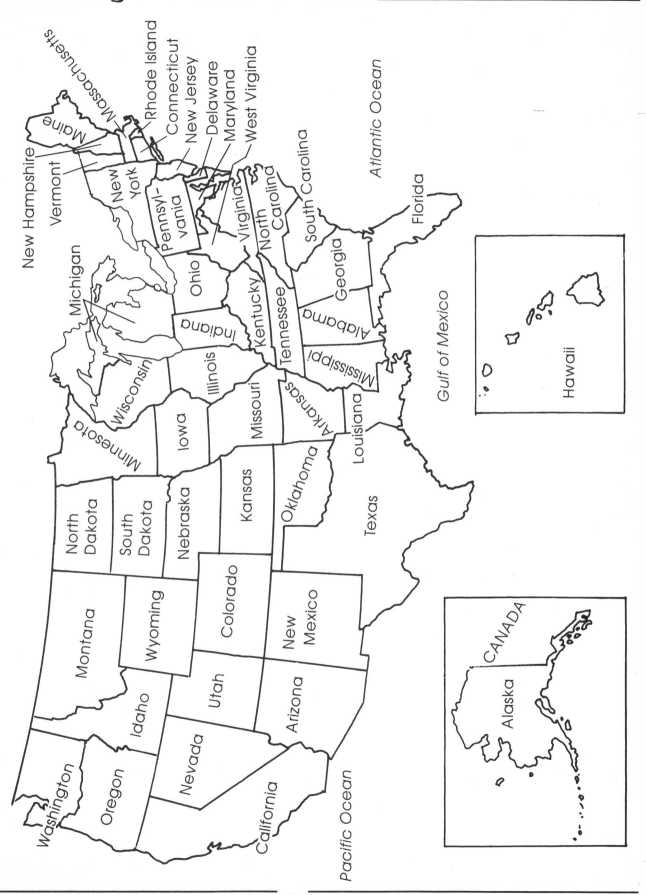

Boundary Bonanza (Continued)   Name _____

Use the map on page 31 to answer these questions about boundaries.

1. Which state is made of islands? _____

2. Which state is S of Utah? _____

3. Which state is NE of Idaho? _____

4. Which state is E of Ohio? _____

5. Which state is NW of Canada? _____

6. Which state lies between Colorado and Missouri? _____

7. Which two states are just S of Michigan? _____

   _____

8. Which states touch New York on its eastern border?

   _____ _____ _____

9. Which state is in the NE corner of the U.S.A.? _____

10. Which state is S of Oklahoma? _____

11. Which states border the Gulf of Mexico? _____ ,

    _____ , _____ , _____ ,

    _____

12. The only state that borders Maine is _____ .

13. Four states that border Texas are _____ , _____ ,

    _____ , and _____ .

14. The state S of North Dakota is _____ .

15. The state SW of Nebraska is _____ .

16. The northwesternmost state is _____ .

River Boundaries

Name _____

Write the number from the map by the name of each river.

____ Colorado River ____ Mississippi River ____ Columbia River

____ Ohio River

Use the map above to answer these questions.

1. The Columbia River forms a natural boundary between these states.

   _____ and _____

2. The Mississippi River forms all or part of the eastern borders of these

   states: _____ , _____ , _____ ,

   _____ , _____

3. The Ohio River forms the southern borders of these states:

   _____ , _____ , _____

4. The Colorado River forms a short border between

   _____ and _____ .

Mystery States

Name _____

Can you name these states? Use a U.S.A. map to identify the shapes. Write the state's name on the line.

1. _____

2. _____

3. _____

4. _____

5. _____

6. _____

7. _____

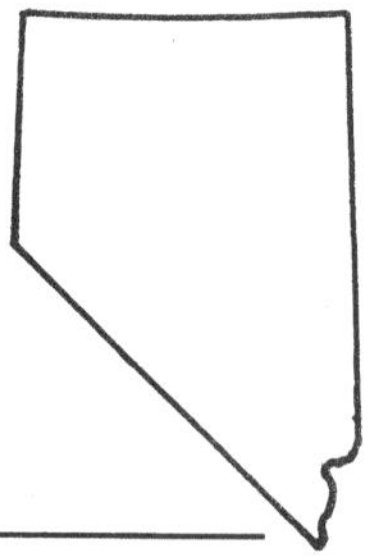

8. _____

9. _____

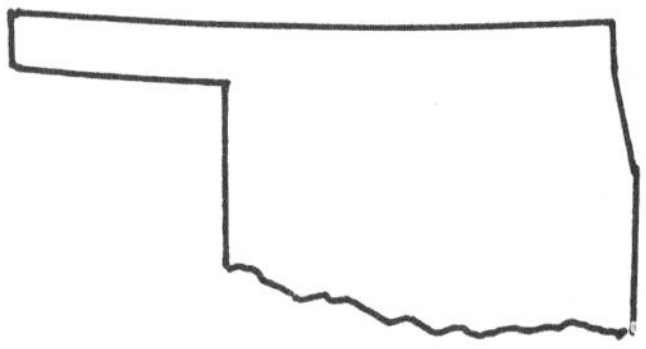

10. _____

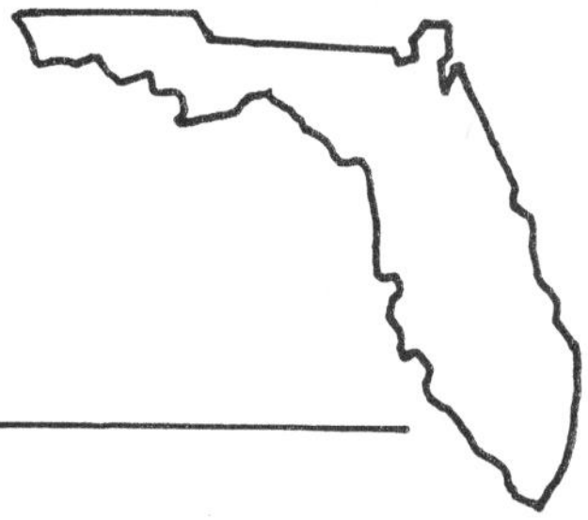

11. _____

12. _____

13. _____

14. _____

15. _____

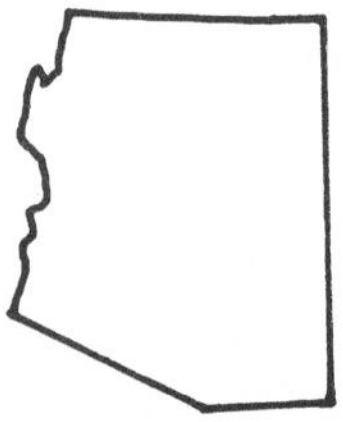

Lateral Movement

Name _____

Lines of latitude on a globe run east and west. They are also called *parallels*. They measure the distance north or south from the equator. Zero degrees latitude (0°) is at the equator. Half of the parallels are north of the equator and half are south of it. The lines do not meet.

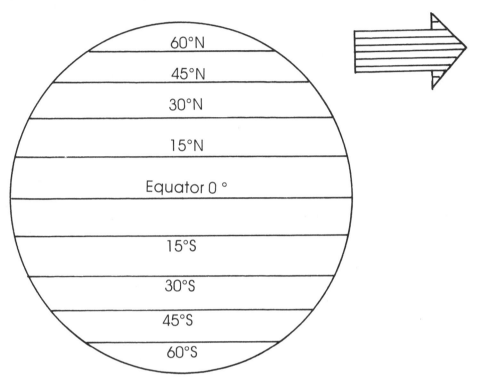

1. What is the symbol for degrees? _____

2. Latitude lines run _____ and _____ .

3. Latitude lines are called _____ .

4. Give the latitude of the equator. _____

5. The parallels above the equator are which direction? _____

6. The parallels below the equator are which direction? _____

7. Color the equator parallel orange.

8. Color 15°N and 15°S green.

9. Color 30°N and 30°S blue.

10. Color 45°N and 45°S red.

11. Color 60°N and 60°S purple.

The Long Lines

Name _____

Lines of longitude on a globe run north and south. They are sometimes called *meridians*. Zero degrees longitude (0°) is an imaginary line called the prime meridian. It passes through Greenwich, England. Half of the lines of longitude are west of the prime meridian, and half are east of it.

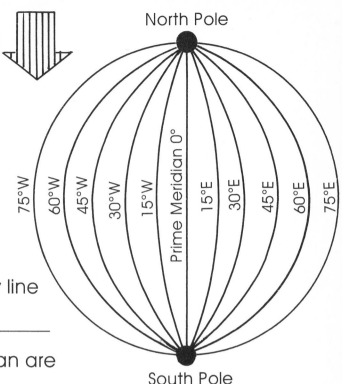

Answer these questions.

1. What is the name for the imaginary line at 0° longitude? _____

2. Lines to the left of the prime meridian are which direction? _____

3. Lines to the right of the prime meridian are which direction? _____

4. Where do lines of longitude come together? _____ and _____

5. Where does the prime meridian pass through?

_____

6. Lines of longitude run in which directions? _____ and

_____

7. Color the prime meridian red.

8. Color the other meridians blue.

 # Merry Meridians

Name _____

Shown on the map are the lines of longitude west of the prime meridian. Answer the questions about these southeastern states.

1. Which two cities lie closest to 90°W?

   _____ , _____

2. To which longitude line is Miami, Florida, closest? _____

3. Which cities lie between 80°W and 85°W? _____ ,

   _____ , _____ , _____

4. Which city is closest to 95°W? _____ _____

5. El Paso, Texas, is closest to which meridian? _____

6. Which two cities are closest to 85°W? _____ , _____

7. Little Rock is between which two meridians? _____ and _____

8. Parts of which states lie between 85°W and 90°W? _____ ,

   _____ , _____ , _____ ,

   _____ , _____ , _____

9. Most of Florida lies between which meridians? _____

10. Corpus Christi lies between which meridians? _____ and _____

Across the U.S.A.

Name _____

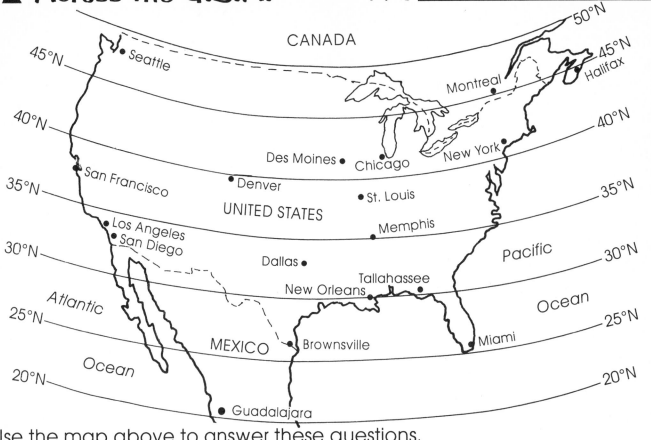

Use the map above to answer these questions.

1. Denver and New York are close to which parallel? _____

2. Which two cities are between 45°N and 50°N? _____ ,

   _____

3. Los Angeles and Memphis are near which parallel? _____

4. Which 3 cities are between parallels 40°N and 45°N?

   _____ , _____ , _____

5. Tallahassee is closest to which parallel? _____

6. St. Louis is between which parallels? _____ and _____

7. Which city is farthest north? _____ It is between which

   parallels? _____ and _____

8. Which city is farthest south? _____ It is between which

   parallels? _____ and _____

9. San Francisco is halfway between _____ and _____ .

See the U.S.A.

Name _____

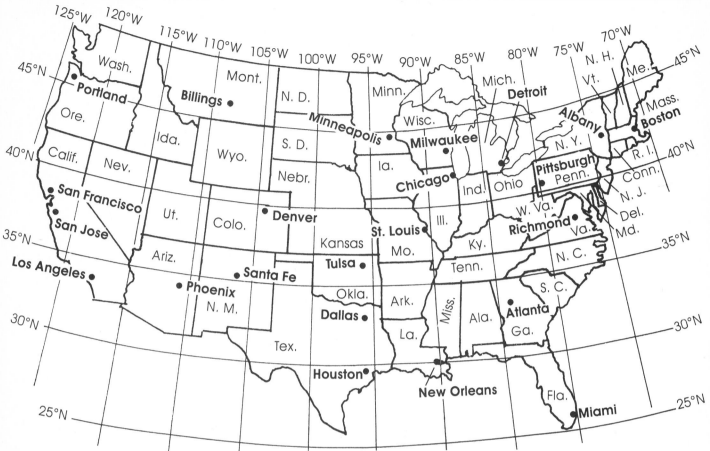

Use the coordinates to plan a trip across the U.S.A. Write the name of the city closest to the intersection.

1. Your trip begins at 40°N–105°W, the Mile High City   _____

2. You fly over the Rocky Mountains to 45°N–125°W   _____

3. Now to 35°N–105°W in New Mexico   _____

4. Next stop is Texas, the city of . . . 30°N–95°W   _____

5. It's Mardi Gras time at 30°N–90°W   _____

6. Then fun in the sun and the Atlantic Ocean 25°N–80°W   _____

7. To the Gateway Arch in the city of . . . 40°N–90°W   _____

8. The Steelers play football here — 40°N–80°W   _____

9. Next to the capital of New York — 40°N–75°W   _____

Picture It!

Name _____

Place a dot at each latitude/longitude coordinate on the graph. Draw lines to connect the dots in order.

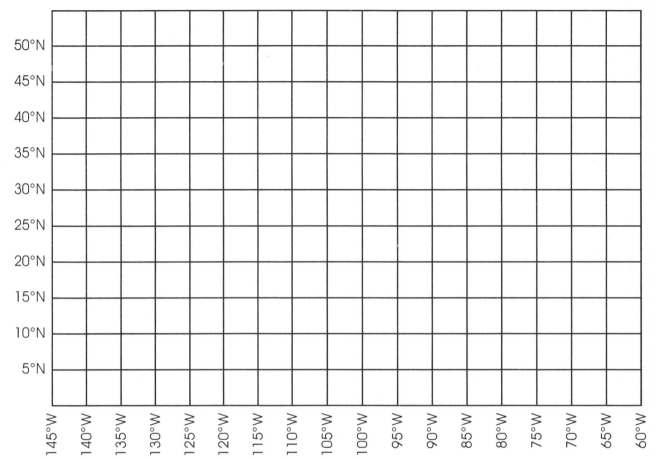

1. 30°N–140°W
2. 25°N–135°W
3. 20°N–130°W
4. 15°N–125°W
5. 15°N–90°W
6. 20°N–85°W

7. 25°N–80°W
8. 30°N–75°W
9. 30°N–90°W
10. 45°N–90°W
11. 45°N–100°W
12. 30°N–100°W

13. 30°N–110°W
14. 45°N–110°W
15. 45°N–120°W
16. 30°N–120°W
17. 30°N–140°W

Now place a yellow **X** at each coordinate below. Do not connect the **X**'s.

1. 45°N–140°W
2. 35°N–135°W

3. 45°N–130°W
4. 40°N–80°W

5. 45°N–70°W
6. 35°N–65°W

Color the rest of the picture.

The Land Down Under

Name _____

We're off to the land of koalas and kangaroos! Write the name of the city closest to the intersection of the latitude/longitude coordinates to locate these places in Australia.

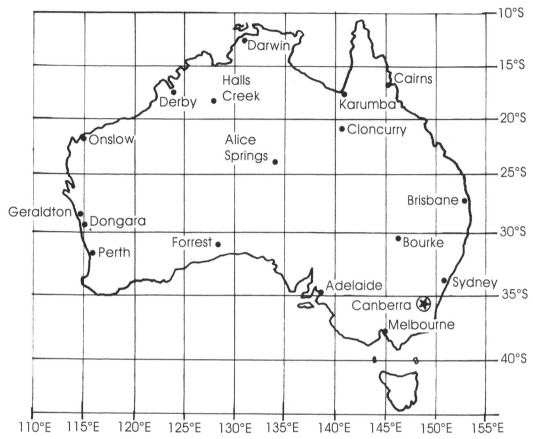

Latitude	Longitude	City
1. 35°S	150°E	
2. 20°S	115°E	
3. 40°S	145°E	
4. 10°S	130°E	
5. 25°S	155°E	
6. 35°S	140°E	
7. 30°S	130°E	
8. 25°S	135°E	

 # State Snatcher

Name _____

The State Snatcher has stolen some of the abbreviations of the states. Write in the missing abbreviations. Use another U.S. map to help you.

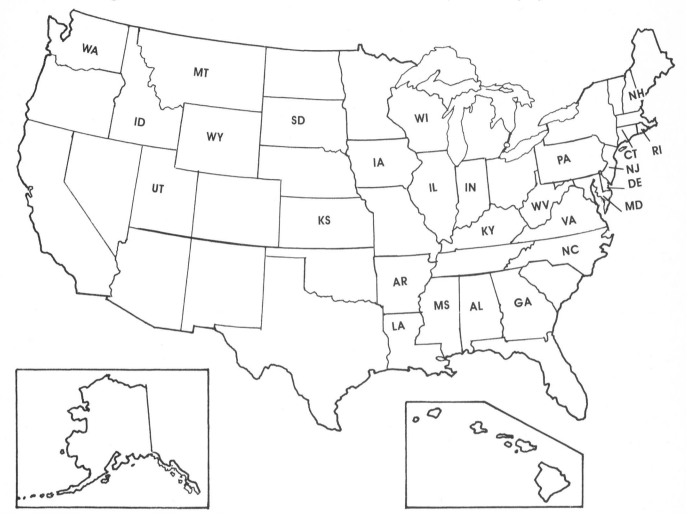

Postal Abbreviations Chart

Alabama	Al	Indiana	IN	Nebraska	NE	South Carolina	SC
Alaska	AK	Iowa	IA	Nevada	NV	South Dakota	SD
Arizona	AZ	Kansas	KS	New Hampshire	NH	Tennessee	TN
Arkansas	AR	Kentucky	KY	New Jersey	NJ	Texas	TX
California	CA	Louisiana	LA	New Mexico	NM	Utah	UT
Colorado	CO	Maine	ME	New York	NY	Vermont	VT
Connecticut	CT	Maryland	MD	North Carolina	NC	Virginia	VA
Delaware	DE	Massachusetts	MA	North Dakota	ND	Washington	WA
Florida	FL	Michigan	MI	Ohio	OH	West Virginia	WV
Georgia	GA	Minnesota	MN	Oklahoma	OK	Wisconsin	WI
Hawaii	HI	Mississippi	MS	Oregon	OR	Wyoming	WY
Idaho	ID	Missouri	MO	Pennsylvania	PA		
Illinois	IL	Montana	MT	Rhode Island	RI		

Map Skills Check-Up

Name _____

How well do you understand map concepts? Test yourself!

1. Name the 7 continents. _____ , _____ ,

   _____ , _____ , _____ ,

   _____ , _____

2. Circle what is usually the map symbol for a national capital.

   •   ★   ⊛   ✳

3. Lines of latitude are called _____ .

4. Circle the globe which shows lines of latitude.

5. 0° latitude is called the _____ .

6. Name the 4 major oceans. _____ , _____ ,

   _____ , _____

7. Lines of longitude are called _____ .

8. 0° longitude is called the _____ .

9. Draw meridians on this circle. Will they be

   lines of latitude or longitude? _____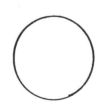

10. What is used on a map to measure distance? _____

11. A spherical map of the earth is called a _____ .

12. Draw the symbol for degrees. _____

13. Label the points of the compass rose.

Answer Key
Grade 3

Which Way Is Up? Name _____

Label the direction each arrow is pointing on the matching line. Use **N, E, S, W, NE, SE, NW, SW**. Then color the arrows as directed in the Color Code Box.

1. E
2. SE
3. W
4. SW

1. S
2. E
3. NE SW
4.

1. N
2. NE
3. E
4. SE
5. SW

1. E
2. E
3. W
4. W
5. SW

1. NE
2. E
3. W
4. W
5. N

1. NE
2. NE
3. S
4. E
5. N

1. E
2. E
3. SW
4. W
5. SW

1. NW
2. N
3. N
4. E
5. S
6. SE

1. E
2. E
3. W
4. S
5. N
6. SW

E
E
S
E
N

Color Code Box

N—red	W—brown
NE—blue	NW—orange
S—green	SW—yellow
SE—pink	E—purple

Page 4

Dizzy Designers Name _____

Decorate the compass rose boxes by following the directions below.

3 green triangles

purple polka dots

2 yellow smiling faces

green diagonal lines

red + blue plaid

red + black stripes

orange wavy lines

two red squares

1. Draw red and black stripes in the **SW** box.
2. Draw 3 green triangles in the **N** box.
3. Make the **E** box red and blue plaid.
4. Draw purple polka dots in the **NW** box.
5. Make orange wavy lines in the **SE** box.
6. Draw two red squares in the **S** box.
7. Draw green diagonal lines in the **W** box.
8. Make two yellow smiling faces in the **NE** box.

Page 5

Space Ship Search Name _____

Gus Galactic needs help in identifying these alien spaceships. Write a ship's letter in each blank to solve these riddles.

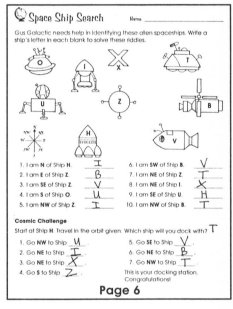

1. I am N of Ship H.   I
2. I am E of Ship Z.   B
3. I am SE of Ship Z.   V
4. I am S of Ship O.   U
5. I am NW of Ship Z.   I

6. I am SW of Ship B.   V
7. I am NE of Ship Z.   T
8. I am NE of Ship I.   X
9. I am SE of Ship U.   H
10. I am NW of Ship B.   T

Cosmic Challenge

Start at Ship H. Travel in the orbit given. Which ship will you dock with? T

1. Go NW to Ship U.
2. Go NE to Ship I.
3. Go NE to Ship X.
4. Go S to Ship Z.
5. Go SE to Ship V.
6. Go NE to Ship B.
7. Go NW to Ship T.

This is your docking station. Congratulations!

Page 6

It's a Strike! Name _____

Don't let these map terms bowl you over! Follow the compass rose directions. Write down the letter on each pin that you bowl down to form a map term. Start with the circled pin.

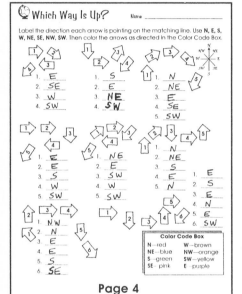

1. Move NE to
2. Move SE to
3. Move SW to
4. Move SW to
5. Move NW to
6. Move NW to

EQUATOR

1. Move SE to
2. Move E to
3. Move NE to
4. Move W to
5. Move NW to
6. Move E to
7. Move E to
8. Move SW to

CONTINENT

1. Move NE to
2. Move E to
3. Move E to
4. Move NE to
5. Move SW to
6. Move NW to
7. Move SW to

LATITUDE

1. Move SE to
2. Move NE to
3. Move SE to
4. Move NE to
5. Move E to
6. Move E to
7. Move SW to
8. Move SW to

LONGITUDE

Page 7

Stocking Sports Shelves Name _____

Identify the grid box location for the following items in the Sports-R-Us Shop.

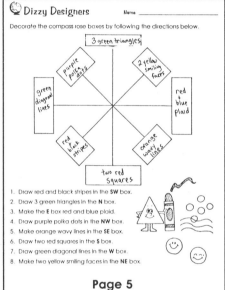

1. golf ball and tee A-4
2. catcher's mitt E-4
3. basketball B-8
4. referee jersey C-5
5. volleyball B-4
6. tennis ball E-8
7. goal post C-1
8. swimming goggles A-7
9. hockey goal net E-3
10. baseball bat C-8

11. whistle A-3
12. cleats A-5
13. golf club D-3
14. tennis racquet D-7
15. football C-2
16. barbell B-2
17. soccer ball E-1
18. hockey stick B-6
19. baseball A-1
20. basketball net D-6

Fill in these grids with your:

D-1 first name   A-8 last name   C-7 favorite sport
C-3 school's name   D-4 favorite number   E-6 favorite color

Page 8

Terrific Treats! Name _____

Create a food map by drawing the foods in the grid as directed.

	1	2	3	4	5	6	7
A	Cheerios	fish	apple	bread	ice-cream bar	French fries	grapes
B	orange	m+ms	grape-fruit	peanut	popcorn	hamburger	candy bar
C	carrot	chocolate kisses	drumstick	pretzel	birthday cake	cupcake	candy cane
D	banana	strawberry	lettuce	lollipop	milk	hot dog	cherry pie
E	pizza	eggs	bacon	ice-cream cone	soda pop	soup	cookie

1. carrot C-1
2. orange B-1
3. pizza E-1
4. birthday cake C-5
5. glass of milk D-5
6. apple A-3
7. chocolate chip cookie E-7
8. hamburger B-6
9. chocolate kisses C-2
10. banana D-1
11. can of soda pop E-5
12. piece of bread A-4
13. candy bar B-7
14. cupcake C-6
15. bacon E-3
16. eggs E-2
17. lollipop D-4
18. ice-cream bar A-5

19. M&Ms B-2
20. Cheerios A-1
21. grapes A-7
22. hot dog D-6
23. head of lettuce D-3
24. cherry pie D-7
25. grapefruit B-3
26. can of soup E-6
27. French fries A-6
28. pretzel C-4
29. peanut B-4
30. drumstick C-3
31. ice-cream cone E-4
32. popcorn B-5
33. fish A-2
34. strawberry D-2
35. candy cane C-7

Page 9

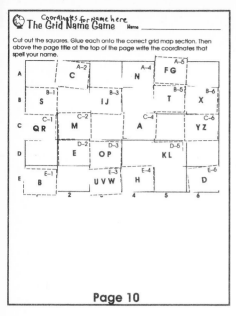

The Grid Name Game

Coordinates for Name here

Name _____

Cut out the squares. Glue each onto the correct grid map section. Then above the page title at the top of the page write the coordinates that spell your name.

Grid with letters: A-2 C, A-4 N, A-5 FG, B-1 S, IJ, B-3, B-5 T, B-6 X, C-1 QR, C-2 M, C-4 A, C-6 YZ, D-2 E, OP, D-3, D-5 KL, E-1 B, E-3 UVW, E-4 H, E-5 D

Page 10

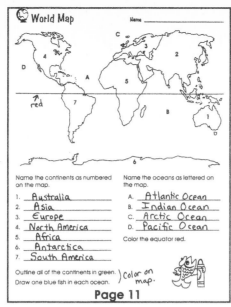

World Map

Name _____

Name the continents as numbered on the map.
1. Australia
2. Asia
3. Europe
4. North America
5. Africa
6. Antarctica
7. South America

Name the oceans as lettered on the map.
A. Atlantic Ocean
B. Indian Ocean
C. Arctic Ocean
D. Pacific Ocean

Color the equator red.

Outline all of the continents in green. Color on map.
Draw one blue fish in each ocean.

Page 11

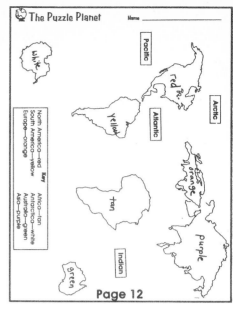

The Puzzle Planet

Name _____

Key
North America—red
South America—yellow
Europe—orange
Africa—tan
Antarctica—white
Australia—green
Asia—purple

Page 12

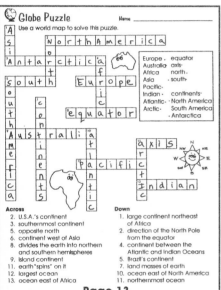

Globe Puzzle

Name _____

Use a world map to solve this puzzle.

Crossword with answers: North America, Antarctica, South, Europe, equator, Australia, axis, Pacific, Indian

Word list:
Europe · equator
Australia · axis
Africa · north
Asia · south
Pacific
Indian · continents
Atlantic · North America
Arctic · South America
· Antarctica

Across
2. U.S.A.'s continent
3. southernmost continent
5. opposite north
6. continent west of Asia
8. divides the earth into northern and southern hemispheres
9. Island continent
11. earth "spins" on it
12. largest ocean
13. ocean east of Africa

Down
1. large continent northeast of Africa
2. direction of the North Pole from the equator
4. continent between the Atlantic and Indian Oceans
5. Brazil's continent
7. land masses of earth
10. ocean east of North America
11. northernmost ocean

Page 13

Global Fun

Name _____

A globe is a model of the earth. Complete the globe by following the directions below.

1. Draw a whale in the southern hemisphere part of the Pacific Ocean.
2. Trace the equator in orange.
3. Draw a shark in the Arctic Ocean.
4. Draw a smile face near Antarctica.
5. Draw an ocean liner in the northern hemisphere part of the Atlantic Ocean.
6. Color the axis poles red.
7. In North America, color Mexico yellow, Canada green, and the U.S.A. red.
8. Draw a yellow X in the northern hemisphere part of Africa.
9. Color Europe purple.
10. Draw rainbow-colored diagonal stripes on South America.
11. Draw orange polka dots on Asia.
12. Draw an orange circle on the southern hemisphere part of Africa.

Page 14

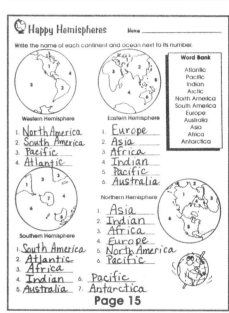

Happy Hemispheres

Name _____

Write the name of each continent and ocean next to its number.

Word Bank
Atlantic
Pacific
Indian
Arctic
North America
South America
Europe
Australia
Asia
Africa
Antarctica

Western Hemisphere
1. North America
2. South America
3. Pacific
4. Atlantic

Eastern Hemisphere
1. Europe
2. Asia
3. Africa
4. Indian
5. Pacific
6. Australia

Northern Hemisphere
1. Asia
2. Indian
3. Africa
4. Europe
5. North America
6. Pacific

Southern Hemisphere
1. South America
2. Atlantic
3. Africa
4. Indian
5. Australia
6. Pacific
7. Antarctica

Page 15

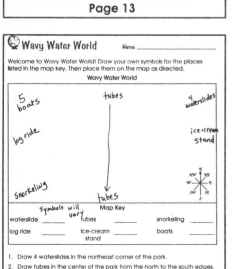

Wavy Water World

Name _____

Welcome to Wavy Water World! Draw your own symbols for the places listed in the map key. Then place them on the map as directed.

Wavy Water World

Symbols will vary. Map Key
waterslide ___ tubes ___ snorkeling ___
log ride ___ ice-cream stand ___ boats ___

1. Draw 4 waterslides in the northeast corner of the park.
2. Draw tubes in the center of the park from the north to the south edges.
3. Draw snorkeling in the southwest corner.
4. Draw the ice-cream stand south of the waterslides.
5. Draw 5 boats in the northwest corner of the park.
6. Draw the log ride on the west side, between boats and snorkeling.

Page 16

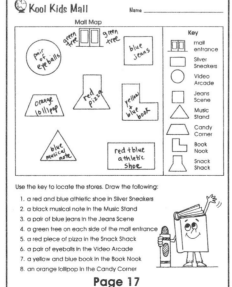

Kool Kids Mall

Name _____

Mall Map

Key
mall entrance
Silver Sneakers
Video Arcade
Jeans Scene
Music Stand
Candy Corner
Book Nook
Snack Shack

Use the key to locate the stores. Draw the following:
1. a red and blue athletic shoe in Silver Sneakers
2. a black musical note in the Music Stand
3. a pair of blue jeans in the Jeans Scene
4. a green tree on each side of the mall entrance
5. a red piece of pizza in the Snack Shack
6. a pair of eyeballs in the Video Arcade
7. a yellow and blue book in the Book Nook
8. an orange lollipop in the Candy Corner

Page 17

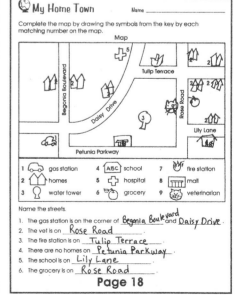

My Home Town

Name _____

Complete the map by drawing the symbols from the key by each matching number on the map.

Map

Key
1 gas station
2 homes
3 water tower
4 school
5 hospital
6 grocery
7 fire station
8 mall
9 veterinarian

Name the streets.
1. The gas station is on the corner of Begonia Boulevard and Daisy Drive
2. The vet is on Rose Road
3. The fire station is on Tulip Terrace
4. There are no homes on Petunia Parkway
5. The school is on Lily Lane
6. The grocery is on Rose Road

Page 18

State Smart

Name _____

Use this map of some of the states to answer the questions below.

Map

Key
- ★ state capital
- • city
- ～ river
- - - - state

1. What state is west of Ohio? **Indiana**
2. The capital of West Virginia is **Charleston**
3. Pittsburgh is a city in the state of **Pennsylvania**
4. What Ohio city is on the Ohio River? **Cincinnati**
5. Which state is southwest of Michigan? **Indiana**
6. What lake is west of Michigan? **Lake Michigan**
7. Frankfort is the capital of **Kentucky**
8. What is the capital of Indiana? **Indianapolis**
9. Springfield is the capital of **Illinois**
10. Chicago is **northeast** of Springfield, Illinois.
11. What Ohio city is northeast of Columbus? **Cleveland**
12. Grand Rapids is **northwest** of Lansing, Michigan.
13. What state is east of Illinois? **Indiana**
14. What lake forms the northern border of Ohio? **Lake Erie**

Page 19

Mixed-Up Map Maker

Name _____

Mattie Map Maker goofed when creating a map of the state of Oopsylvania. Circle in color her mistakes and put a number by each one. Then describe each error on the line with the matching number. (**Hint:** The key shows the correct map symbols.)

Oopsylvania Map

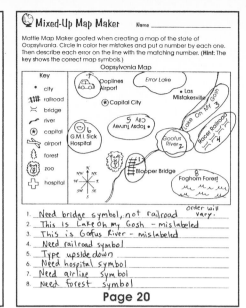

order will vary.

1. Need bridge symbol, not railroad
2. This is Lake Oh my Gosh - mislabeled
3. This is Goofus River - mislabeled
4. Need railroad symbol
5. Type upside down
6. Need hospital symbol
7. Need airline symbol
8. Need forest symbol

Page 20

Creating a Map

Name _____

Pretend you are looking at your school classroom from high atop the lighting fixtures. Draw how your classroom looks. Include a key to explain the symbols you draw.

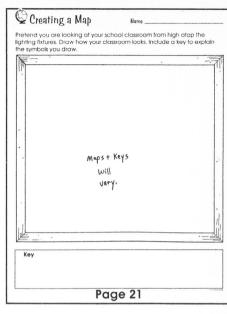

Maps + Keys will vary.

Key

Page 21

Delivery Dilemma

Name _____

Carrie lost her way while delivering the mail. Follow the directions to help her complete her route.

Carrie's Map

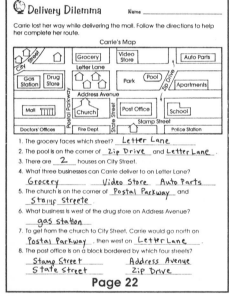

1. The grocery faces which street? **Letter Lane**
2. The pool is on the corner of **Zip Drive** and **Letter Lane**
3. There are **2** houses on City Street.
4. What three businesses can Carrie deliver to on Letter Lane?
   Grocery **Video Store** **Auto Parts**
5. The church is on the corner of **Postal Parkway** and **Stamp Streete**
6. What business is west of the drug store on Address Avenue?
   gas station
7. To get from the church to City Street, Carrie would go north on **Postal Parkway**, then west on **Letter Lane**
8. The post office is on a block bordered by which four streets?
   Stamp Street **Address Avenue**
   State street **Zip Drive**

Page 22

A Real "Moose-tery"

Name _____

Horrible Harvey Hunter has disappeared somewhere in the Mysterious Moosehead Mansion. Detective Dimwitt is trying to find him. Use the key to identify rooms in the mansion. Then use a pencil to trace the route Detective Dimwitt took to locate the hapless Harvey. *Students may or may not label rooms*

Moosehead Mansion Map

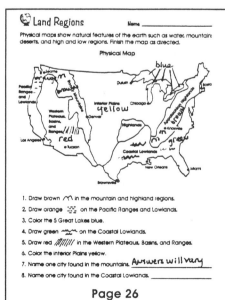

Key
1—Main Entrance
2—Antler Atrium
3—Haunted Hoot Room
4—Moosehead Trophy Room
5—Frightful Family Room
6—Graceless Gallery
7—Moosetrack Gym
8—Master Moose Suite
9—Spooky Spa
10—Scary Library

Detective Dimwitt's Route

1. He enters the mansion at the Main Entrance.
2. Next he checks out the Moosetrack Gym.
3. Then he sneaks down the hall to the Antler Atrium.
4. From there he checks the Spooky Spa.
5. No luck, so on to the Scary Library he goes.
6. Next, the detective scans the Moosehead Trophy Room.
7. Then he walks along the hall to look in the Frightful Family Room.
8. No Harvey there, so he moves on to the Graceless Gallery.
9. Could he be in the Master Moose Suite? He checks there.
10. Then he looks in the Haunted Hoot Room.
11. There he discovers a secret room. Inside he finds Harvey reading a hunting magazine. The search is over!

Page 23

Color My World

Name _____

Color each gumball as directed in the Color Key.

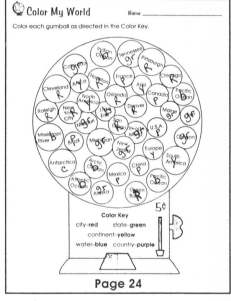

Color Key
- city–red state–green
- continent–yellow
- water–blue country–purple

Page 24

Natural Wonders

Name _____

Earth's physical features are its natural formations. Match each formation with its definition by writing a number in each blank.

- **8** river
- **4** bay
- **2** island
- **11** gulf
- **1** mountain
- **9** plain
- **6** lake
- **3** peninsula
- **7** valley
- **5** volcano
- **10** ocean

1. land rising high above the land around it
2. land surrounded completely by water
3. piece of land surrounded by water on all but one side
4. inlet of a large water body that extends into the land; smaller than a gulf
5. Earth opening that spills lava, rock, and gases
6. large inland body of water
7. lowland between hills or mountains
8. long, narrow body of water
9. large area of flat grasslands
10. vast body of salt water
11. large area of a sea or ocean partially enclosed by land

Now write each feature's number on the map.

Features Map

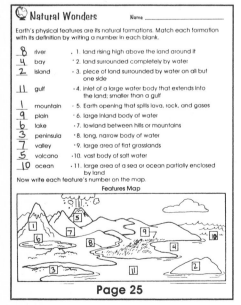

Page 25

Land Regions

Name _____

Physical maps show natural features of the earth such as water, mountains, deserts, and high and low regions. Finish the map as directed.

Physical Map

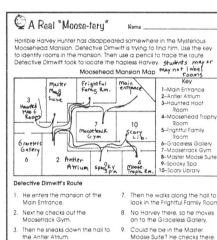

1. Draw brown ⋏⋏ in the mountain and highland regions.
2. Draw orange ⋮⋮⋮ on the Pacific Ranges and Lowlands.
3. Color the 5 Great Lakes blue.
4. Draw green ～～ on the Coastal Lowlands.
5. Draw red ///////// in the Western Plateaus, Basins, and Ranges.
6. Color the Interior Plains yellow.
7. Name one city found in the mountains. **Answers will vary**
8. Name one city found in the Coastal Lowlands.

Page 26

Northern Neighbors

Name _____

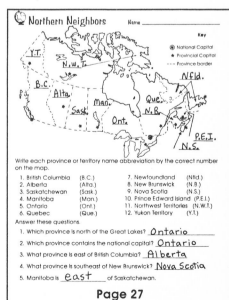

Key
- ◉ National Capital
- ★ Provincial Capital
- - - - Province border

Write each province or territory name abbreviation by the correct number on the map.

1. British Columbia (B.C.)
2. Alberta (Alta.)
3. Saskatchewan (Sask.)
4. Manitoba (Man.)
5. Ontario (Ont.)
6. Quebec (Que.)
7. Newfoundland (Nfld.)
8. New Brunswick (N.B.)
9. Nova Scotia (N.S.)
10. Prince Edward Island (P.E.I.)
11. Northwest Territories (N.W.T.)
12. Yukon Territory (Y.T.)

Answer these questions.

1. Which province is north of the Great Lakes? **Ontario**
2. Which province contains the national capital? **Ontario**
3. What province is east of British Columbia? **Alberta**
4. What province is southeast of New Brunswick? **Nova Scotia**
5. Manitoba is **east** of Saskatchewan.

Page 27

Scale Is Fun!　Name _____

A scale measures distance on a map. Use the scale given to measure distances in this winter wonderland. Cut out the ruler. Use it to measure from ✳ to ✳ to answer the questions below.

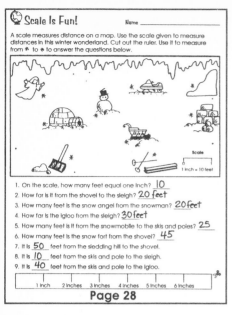

Scale
1 inch = 10 feet

1. On the scale, how many feet equal one inch? **10**
2. How far is it from the shovel to the sleigh? **20 feet**
3. How many feet is the snow angel from the snowman? **20 feet**
4. How far is the igloo from the sleigh? **30 feet**
5. How many feet is it from the snowmobile to the skis and poles? **25**
6. How many feet is the snow fort from the shovel? **45**
7. It is **50** feet from the sledding hill to the shovel.
8. It is **10** feet from the skis and pole to the sleigh.
9. It is **40** feet from the skis and pole to the igloo.

| 1 inch | 2 inches | 3 inches | 4 inches | 5 inches | 6 inches |

Page 28

New Neighbors for Nelly　Name _____

Nelly and her family have just moved to their new farm. How far will Nelly have to travel to meet her new neighbors? Cut out the ruler and use to measure the distances. Be sure to check the scale given on the map. Measure from • to •.

Nelly's Map

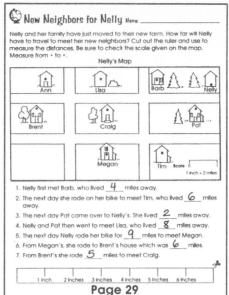

Scale
1 inch = 2 miles

1. Nelly first met Barb, who lived **4** miles away.
2. The next day she rode on her bike to meet Tim, who lived **6** miles away.
3. The next day Pat came over to Nelly's. She lived **2** miles away.
4. Nelly and Pat then went to meet Lisa, who lived **8** miles away.
5. The next day Nelly rode her bike for **9** miles to meet Megan.
6. From Megan's, she rode to Brent's house which was **6** miles.
7. From Brent's she rode **5** miles to meet Craig.

| 1 inch | 2 inches | 3 inches | 4 inches | 5 inches | 6 inches |

Page 29

Flight Path Frenzy　Name _____

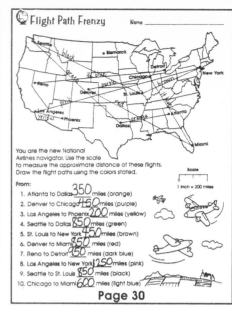

You are the new National Airlines navigator. Use the scale to measure the approximate distance of these flights. Draw the flight paths using the colors stated.

Scale
1 inch = 200 miles

From:
1. Atlanta to Dallas **350** miles (orange)
2. Denver to Chicago **450** miles (purple)
3. Los Angeles to Phoenix **200** miles (yellow)
4. Seattle to Dallas **850** miles (green)
5. St. Louis to New York **750** miles (brown)
6. Denver to Miami **850** miles (red)
7. Reno to Detroit **450** miles (dark blue)
8. Los Angeles to New York **250** miles (pink)
9. Seattle to St. Louis **850** miles (black)
10. Chicago to Miami **600** miles (light blue)

Page 30

Boundary Bonanza　Name _____

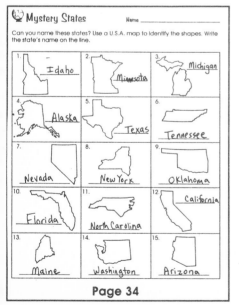

Page 31

Boundary Bonanza (Continued)　Name _____

Use the map on page 31 to answer these questions about boundaries.
1. Which state is made of islands? **Hawaii**
2. Which state is S of Utah? **Arizona**
3. Which state is NE of Idaho? **Montana**
4. Which state is E of Ohio? **Pennsylvania**
5. Which state is NW of Canada? **Alaska**
6. Which state lies between Colorado and Missouri? **Kansas**
7. Which two states are just S of Michigan? **Indiana Ohio**
8. Which states touch New York on its eastern border? **Vermont Massachusetts Connecticut**
9. Which state is in the NE corner of the U.S.A.? **Maine**
10. Which state is S of Oklahoma? **Texas**
11. Which states border the Gulf of Mexico? **Texas Louisiana Mississippi Alabama Florida**
12. The only state that borders Maine is **New Hampshire**
13. Four states that border Texas are **New Mexico Oklahoma Arkansas**, and **Louisiana**
14. The state S of North Dakota is **South Dakota**
15. The state SW of Nebraska is **Colorado**
16. The northwesternmost state is **Washington**

Page 32

River Boundaries　Name _____

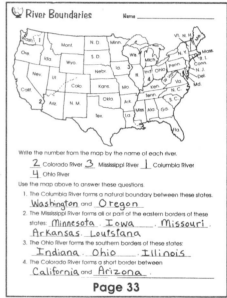

Write the number from the map by the name of each river.
2 Colorado River　**3** Mississippi River　**1** Columbia River
4 Ohio River

Use the map above to answer these questions.
1. The Columbia River forms a natural boundary between these states. **Washington** and **Oregon**
2. The Mississippi River forms all or part of the eastern borders of these states: **Minnesota, Iowa, Missouri, Arkansas, Louisiana**
3. The Ohio River forms the southern borders of these states: **Indiana, Ohio, Illinois**
4. The Colorado River forms a short border between **California** and **Arizona**

Page 33

Mystery States　Name _____

Can you name these states? Use a U.S.A. map to identify the shapes. Write the state's name on the line.

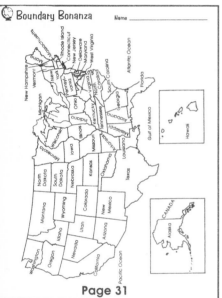

1. **Idaho**
2. **Minnesota**
3. **Michigan**
4. **Alaska**
5. **Texas**
6. **Tennessee**
7. **Nevada**
8. **New York**
9. **Oklahoma**
10. **Florida**
11. **North Carolina**
12. **California**
13. **Maine**
14. **Washington**
15. **Arizona**

Page 34

Lateral Movement　Name _____

Lines of latitude on a globe run east and west. They are also called *parallels*. They measure the distance north or south from the equator. Zero degrees latitude (0°) is at the equator. Half of the parallels are north of the equator and half are south of it. The lines do not meet.

1. What is the symbol for degrees? **°**
2. Latitude lines run **east** and **west**
3. Latitude lines are called **parallels**
4. Give the latitude of the equator. **0°**
5. The parallels above the equator are which direction? **north**
6. The parallels below the equator are which direction? **south**
7. Color the equator parallel orange.
8. Color 15°N and 15°S green.
9. Color 30°N and 30°S blue.
10. Color 45°N and 45°S red.
11. Color 60°N and 60°S purple.

Page 35

The Long Lines　Name _____

Lines of longitude on a globe run north and south. They are sometimes called *meridians*. Zero degrees longitude (0°) is an imaginary line called the prime meridian. It passes through Greenwich, England. Half of the lines of longitude are west of the prime meridian, and half are east of it.

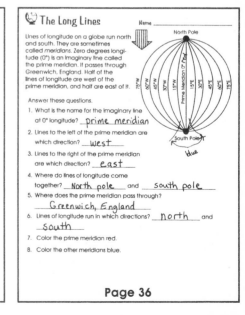

Answer these questions.
1. What is the name for the imaginary line at 0° longitude? **prime meridian**
2. Lines to the left of the prime meridian are which direction? **west**
3. Lines to the right of the prime meridian are which direction? **east**
4. Where do lines of longitude come together? **North pole** and **south pole**
5. Where does the prime meridian pass through? **Greenwich, England**
6. Lines of longitude run in which directions? **north** and **south**
7. Color the prime meridian red.
8. Color the other meridians blue.

Page 36

Merry Meridians

Name _____

Shown on the map are the lines of longitude west of the prime meridian. Answer the questions about these southeastern states.

1. Which two cities lie closest to 90°W?
   Jackson, New Orleans
2. To which longitude line is Miami, Florida, closest? 80°W
3. Which cities lie between 80°W and 85°W? Atlanta,
   Charleston, Tallahassee, Miami
4. Which city is closest to 95°W? Tulsa
5. El Paso, Texas, is closest to which meridian? 105°W
6. Which two cities are closest to 85°W? Atlanta, Tallahassee
7. Little Rock is between which two meridians? 95°W and 90°W
8. Parts of which states lie between 85°W and 90°W? Florida,
   Georgia, Alabama, Mississippi,
   Tennessee, Arkansas, Louisiana
9. Most of Florida lies between which meridians? 85°W and 80°W
10. Corpus Christi lies between which meridians? 100°W and 95°W

Page 37

Across the U.S.A.

Name _____

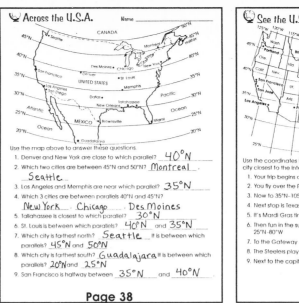

Use the map above to answer these questions.

1. Denver and New York are close to which parallel? 40°N
2. Which two cities are between 45°N and 50°N? Montreal,
   Seattle
3. Los Angeles and Memphis are near which parallel? 35°N
4. Which 3 cities are between parallels 40°N and 45°N?
   New York, Chicago, Des Moines
5. Tallahassee is closest to which parallel? 30°N
6. St. Louis is between which parallels? 40°N and 35°N
7. Which city is farthest north? Seattle It is between which
   parallels? 45°N and 50°N
8. Which city is farthest south? Guadalajara It is between which
   parallels? 20°N and 25°N
9. San Francisco is halfway between 35°N and 40°N

Page 38

See the U.S.A.

Name _____

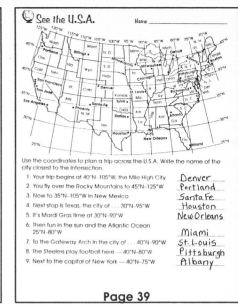

Use the coordinates to plan a trip across the U.S.A. Write the name of the city closest to the intersection.

1. Your trip begins at 40°N-105°W, the Mile High City
2. You fly over the Rocky Mountains to 45°N-125°W
3. Now to 35°N-105°W in New Mexico
4. Next stop is Texas, the city of . . . 30°N-95°W
5. It's Mardi Gras time at 30°N-90°W
6. Then fun in the sun and the Atlantic Ocean 25°N-80°W
7. To the Gateway Arch in the city of . . . 40°N-90°W
8. The Steelers play football here --- 40°N-80°W
9. Next to the capital of New York --- 40°N-75°W

Denver
Portland
Santa Fe
Houston
New Orleans

Miami
St. Louis
Pittsburgh
Albany

Page 39

Picture It!

Name _____

Place a dot at each latitude/longitude coordinate on the graph. Draw lines to connect the dots in order.

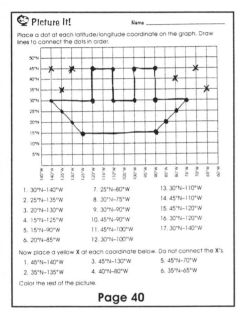

1. 30°N–140°W
2. 25°N–135°W
3. 20°N–130°W
4. 15°N–125°W
5. 15°N–90°W
6. 20°N–85°W
7. 25°N–80°W
8. 30°N–75°W
9. 30°N–90°W
10. 45°N–90°W
11. 45°N–100°W
12. 30°N–100°W
13. 30°N–110°W
14. 45°N–110°W
15. 45°N–120°W
16. 30°N–120°W
17. 30°N–140°W

Now place a yellow X at each coordinate below. Do not connect the X's.

1. 45°N–140°W
2. 35°N–135°W
3. 45°N–130°W
4. 40°N–80°W
5. 45°N–70°W
6. 35°N–65°W

Color the rest of the picture.

Page 40

The Land Down Under

Name _____

We're off to the land of koalas and kangaroos! Write the name of the city closest to the intersection of the latitude/longitude coordinates to locate these places in Australia.

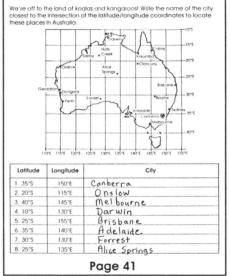

	Latitude	Longitude	City
1.	35°S	150°E	Canberra
2.	20°S	115°E	Onslow
3.	40°S	145°E	Melbourne
4.	10°S	130°E	Darwin
5.	25°S	155°E	Brisbane
6.	35°S	140°E	Adelaide
7.	30°S	130°E	Forrest
8.	25°S	135°E	Alice Springs

Page 41

State Snatcher

Name _____

The State Snatcher has stolen some of the abbreviations of the states. Write in the missing abbreviations. Use another U.S. map to help you.

Postal Abbreviations Chart

Alabama	AL	Indiana	IN	Nebraska	NE
Alaska	AK	Iowa	IA	Nevada	NV
Arizona	AZ	Kansas	KS	New Hampshire	NH
Arkansas	AR	Kentucky	KY	New Jersey	NJ
California	CA	Louisiana	LA	New Mexico	NM
Colorado	CO	Maine	ME	New York	NY
Connecticut	CT	Maryland	MD	North Carolina	NC
Delaware	DE	Massachusetts	MA	North Dakota	ND
Florida	FL	Michigan	MI	Ohio	OH
Georgia	GA	Minnesota	MN	Oklahoma	OK
Hawaii	HI	Mississippi	MS	Oregon	OR
Idaho	ID	Missouri	MO	Pennsylvania	PA
Illinois	IL	Montana	MT	Rhode Island	RI

South Carolina	SC
South Dakota	SD
Tennessee	TN
Texas	TX
Utah	UT
Vermont	VT
Virginia	VA
Washington	WA
West Virginia	WV
Wisconsin	WI
Wyoming	WY

Page 42

Map Skills Check-Up

Name _____

How well do you understand map concepts? Test yourself!

1. Name the 7 continents North America, South America,
   Europe, Asia, Australia,
   Africa, Antarctica
2. Circle what is usually the map symbol for a national capital.
   •   *   (⊛)   *
3. Lines of latitude are called parallels
4. Circle the globe which shows lines of latitude.
5. 0° latitude is called the equator
6. Name the 4 major oceans. Pacific, Atlantic,
   Indian, Arctic
7. Lines of longitude are called meridians
8. 0° longitude is called the prime meridian
9. Draw meridians on this circle. Will they be
   lines of latitude or longitude? longitude
10. What is used on a map to measure distance? scale
11. A spherical map of the earth is called a globe
12. Draw the symbol for degrees. °
13. Label the points of the compass rose.

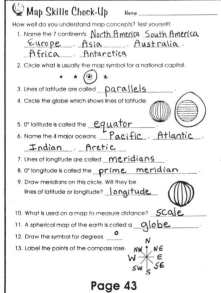

Page 43

IF5190 *Map Skills*